The Little Things in Life

Quilted Projects to Brighten Your Day

By Heather and Elissa Willms

Title: The Little Things in Life
Subtitle: Quilted Projects to Brighten Your Day
By Heather and Elissa Willms

Editor: Kent Richards
Designer: Sarah Meiers
Photography: Aaron T. Leimkuehler
Illustration: Eric Sears
Technical Editor: Lisa Calle
Photo Editor: Jo Ann Groves

Published by:
Kansas City Star Books
1729 Grand Blvd.
Kansas City, Missouri, USA 64108

Kansas City Star Quilts moves quickly to publicize corrections to our books. You can find corrections at www.KansasCityStarQuilts.com, then click on "Corrections."

First edition, first printing
ISBN: 978-1-61169-129-0
Library of Congress Control Number: 2014939090

Printed in the United States of America by Walsworth Publishing Co., Marceline, MO

KANSAS CITY STAR
QUILTS
Continuing the Tradition
KansasCityStarQuilts.com

To order copies, call StarInfo
at (816) 234-4473.

Table of Contents

In loving memory
of Dad
and Grandpa
John Booth
(1933–2014)

Introduction

It is often the little things in life that make or break our day. A smile, a kind word of encouragement or sunshine after days of rain can lift our spirits and put a bounce in our step. This book contains some of our favorite little things, made with our favorite little tools, in our favorite place to be (our studio). We hope that you will enjoy creating the little projects in this book and hopefully make someone else's day a little bit brighter when you share them as gifts.

Elissa and Heather

Skill level ratings:

I have done quite a bit of sewing and quilting — bring it on!

I can find my way around a sewing machine and can read a pattern all by myself.

I have done a lot of quilting and sewing and should be on Project Runway.

All seam allowances are ¼" unless otherwise noted. Yardage requirements are based on 40" wide fabric. Please read all instructions before starting a project.

Project Inspiration Gallery

Favorite Little Things in Our Studio

Buttons — You will notice that almost every project in this book has a button attached somewhere. Buttons are one of the little things in life that add whimsy to a project. In our studio, there is a row of button jars behind Elissa's long arm. These jars not only look great, but we are constantly digging through the jars to find that "perfect" button.

We purchase buttons wherever we find them. If you are lucky enough to stumble onto a button jar or bag at a thrift store or garage sale, you have truly found a treasure. We love the buttons that are hand dyed by Hillcreek Buttons. They come in a wide variety of colors and sizes, and we like that they can be purchased in one color or a mixture of colors.

Fray Check — A discussion of buttons leads us directly to Fray Check. This awesome product is used most often in our studio when attaching buttons. Once the buttons have been sewn onto a project, dab a drop of Fray Check onto the thread that is used to sew the button in place. This strengthens the relationship between the button and the project, thus helping to prevent button loss.

Bohin Marking Pens — These are hands down our favorite marking tools, and they are never far from reach and truly are erasable. Sadly, not all marking tools that make this claim are actually erasable. The chalk is very fine, which makes it excellent for precise marking. The gentlemen from Bohen are awesome to chat with and it is a must-visit booth for us at International Quilt Market each year.

Bohin Seam Rippers — Besides being delicious to look at, these seam rippers are fine and sharp. The fold-away blade makes them compact and safe for trips outside of the studio, as well as safe when little people are close at hand.

Clover Appliqué Pins — We love using Clover Appliqué pins as they are small and sharp. Their short length helps to minimize thread tangles and allows the quilter to pin small shapes to the background fabric.

Clover Bias Tape Makers — If you do not have these little gems, you must rush out and purchase at least one! Heather thought making bias tape would be a royal pain before trying out a Clover Bias Tape Maker. Now we wonder how we lived without them. They are easy to use and make your projects look custom made (which of course they are) because you can coordinate the bias tape fabric with the fabrics used in the rest of your project!

Heavy Weight Cotton Fabric — Every time we head to International Quilt Market, Elissa comes home with new heavy weight cotton. Many fabric companies are starting to add this weight of fabric to their collections. The weight of the cotton adds stability and durability to a project, and although they are not suitable for all projects, throughout the book we do mention when they would be ideal.

Annie's Soft and Stable — How have we lived without this stuff? When we published our bag book, someone asked us if we had tried Soft and Stable. We had not, but our curiosity was piqued. It is an amazing product for projects that need a firm surface or base. It is highly recommended for "Lunch To Go," "Brewed With Taste" and "The Stylish Techy."

Contemporary Reversible Apron

Finished Size: 22" × 29½" (excluding ties)

Skill Level:

The birth of the apron is lost to history, but we all know its many purposes over the years!

Besides protecting clothes during cooking and housework, it was used to wipe away tears, carry eggs from the chicken coop to the house, polish cutlery, dry hands and it was often waved from the porch to call everyone in to supper.

The apron is enjoying a revival recently. With so many awesome fabrics to choose from, you can make a unique apron perfect for yourself and your friends and family!

Because this is a reversible apron, when selecting fabric lay the front and back prints wrong sides together and check that one print does not show through to the other side of the apron.

Instructions given are for the black and white version of the apron. Sewing a garment is a little different from quilting. Keep the following things in mind as you sew: Backstitch at the beginning and end of each seam and topstitching seam, and all seams are ¼" unless otherwise noted (which we know is contrary to garment sewing and more like quilting).

We've used contrasting thread to add a pop to the topstitching on our apron.

PROJECT INSPIRATION

CONTEMPORARY REVERSIBLE APRON

Materials

- ½ yard (.5m) of white floral print for apron front
- ¾ yard (.7m) of white geometric print* for apron back
- ⅓ yard (.3m) of black geometric print for front panel
- ½ yard of black polka dot print for waistband and ties
- 4" × 25" of lightweight fusible interfacing
- Three ⅝" black buttons, two ½" black buttons and six ⅜" buttons
- Scraps of colored fabric prints for appliquéd circles
- Freezer paper or Steam-A-Seam for circle appliqué
- Fray Check

We recommend a fairly busy print in a coordinating color for the back of the apron so that the thread is hidden when sewing on the buttons.

Cutting

From white floral print for apron front, cut:
1 — 14½" × 29½"

From white geometric print for apron back, cut:
1 — 20½" × 29½"

From black geometric print for front panel print, cut:
1 — 7½" × 29½"

From black polka dot for waistband and tie, cut:
1 — 5½" × 22" for waistband
2 — 5½" × width of fabric for ties

Preparing the Apron Skirt

1. Prepare circle templates for the front panel and waist-band using the appliqué method of your choice. We chose to needle turn our circles, and therefore used freezer paper to prepare the circles. You will need 3 large, 2 medium and 4 small circles for the front panel and 2 small circles for the waistband. Circle templates can be found on page 16.

2. Lay out the front panel circles on the 7½" × 29½" black geometric rectangle and find an arrangement that you find pleasing. Appliqué the circles in place using the appliqué method of your choice. Do not sew the buttons on at this point. Do not appliqué the circles within 1½" of the edge of the panel to allow room for the seams.

3. Sew the front panel to the bottom of the 14½" × 29½" white floral print of apron front, sewing along the 29½" side. Sew the white geometric print for the apron back to the bottom of the front panel to create one large rectangle. Press both seams toward front panel. Ensure that directional fabrics are correctly aligned.

Note: If you are using directional prints, the print should be upright above the circle panel and upside down below the circle panel as the back of the apron (or bottom rectangle) will be folded up to the reverse side of the apron during construction.

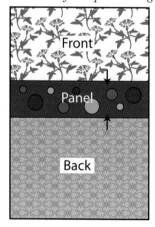

4. Fold the rectangle in half, right sides together so that the raw edges of the front and back panel are aligned opposite the fold. Sew along the two outside edges of the apron. Clip corners and turn right side out. Press. When the apron is turned right side out, a ½" black strip from the front panel will be wrapped around to the back to create the bottom trim on the back of the apron.

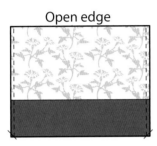

Open edge

5. Topstitch along both sides of the apron a scant ¼" from the side edges. Remember to backstitch when starting and ending each topstitching seam.

Waistband and Ties

1. Fold a 5½" × 40" tie rectangle in half along the length of the strip. Using a rotary cutter and ruler, cut a 60 degree angle at one end of the strip. For easy turning, have the narrow end of the diagonal cut along the fold line.

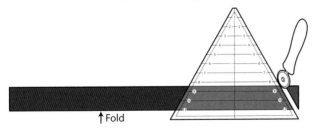

↑ Fold

2. Sew a ¼" seam along the length of the strip and down the diagonal side. You will be leaving the short, square end of the strip open. Clip corners and turn. Press. Topstitch around the outside edge of the tie, stitching a scant ¼" away from the edge. Repeat for the second tie. Set aside.

Clip

↑ Fold

3. On the waistband, position and appliqué a small pink circle on the bottom right side of the band, 4½" from the right side of the band and ¾" from the bottom of the band. Repeat with the remaining small white circle on the top left side of the band, 4½" from the left side of the band and ¾" from the top of the band.

¾" 4½"

¾"

4½"

4. Cut a piece of lightweight interfacing 2 ¾" × 22". Fuse to the wrong side of the waistband, aligning the length of the interfacing with the bottom half of the waistband.

Interfacing

5. Fold the top edge of the waistband over ¼", wrong sides together. Press.

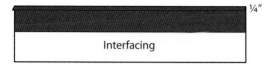

6. Pin the top open edges of the apron together. Baste two lines of stitching a scant ⅜" and ⅝" from the raw edges of the top of the apron. Leave long thread tails without backstitching at the beginning and end of basting to pull up gathers.

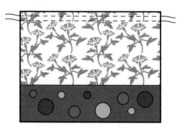

7. Lay the apron top along the bottom side of the waistband (the edge where the interfacing is), right sides together (the apron front should be facing the waistband). Pin the two pieces together, with a ½" of the waistband extending beyond each edge of the apron skirt. Place the pins so they are perpendicular to the top edge of the apron.

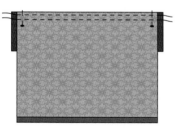

8. Wrap the two top left basting threads on the back side of the apron (one from each basting line) around the pin at the left side of the apron to secure the basting threads. Wrap the threads in a figure-eight pattern around the pin.

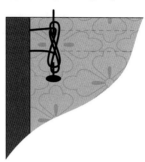

9. Pick up the top basting threads from the right side of the apron and gently pull the two threads together to gather the top edge of the apron. Pull the threads until the apron top fits the waistband, making the gathers as even as possible. Wrap these gathering threads around the right pin using the same figure-eight pattern to secure the gathering threads. Even out the gathers along the apron skirt and pin the remainder of the apron skirt to the waistband.

10. Stitch the apron skirt to the waistband using a ½" seam. Press seam allowance toward the waistband. Remove any visible gathering stitches.

11. Working with one tie at a time, prepare and add the ties as follows: On the open end of the tie, mark the middle of the tie and ½" from each outer edge of the tie using a pin or marking tool.

12. Pull the two outside marks to the center mark to form a pleat. Pin. Baste ¼" from the end of the tie to hold the pleat in place. Repeat with second tie making sure that the angle at the end of the tie is the opposite of the first tie, so that they match when they are sewn on to each side of the apron.

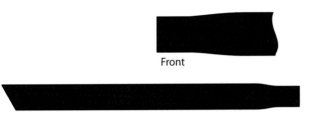

Front   Back

13. With right sides together, pin the ties to the front of the waistband (closest to the apron skirt), positioning the bottom of each tie ½" from the seam line of the apron skirt. The unfinished edge of the tie must align with the side of the waistband. The front side of the pleat should be facing the right side of the waistband. Pin in place.

14. Fold the waistband in half along the length of the band, right sides together. The folded edge of the waistband (step 4) should line up with the bottom edge of the waistband (which you have just sewn to the apron skirt).

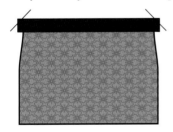

15. Sew a ½" seam along both sides of the apron waistband, making sure that the ties and the turned up ¼" seam are sewn into the seam. Trim seam allowances to ¼", clip corners and turn waistband right sides out. Press. See diagram from step 14.

16. Using a slip stitch, hand stitch the folded edge of apron waistband to the apron. Press. Topstitch around the apron waistband, stitching ⅛" from the outside edge.

Attaching the Buttons

Sew a button onto each appliqué circle. Sew a ⅝" button onto each 2⅞" diameter circle, a ½" button onto each 2" diameter circle and a ⅜" button onto each 1½" diameter circle. We offset our buttons for a more whimsical look. Add a dab of Fray Check to the thread that attaches each button to the apron skirt to further secure the button.

Although you may see the button thread on the back side of the apron, we feel it is important to sew the buttons on at the end of the apron construction to help hold the two layers of the apron skirt together. This is why we chose a fairly busy print for our apron front and back and two fabrics that were color coordinated.

If you would like to further attach the front and back of the apron skirt, topstitch along the edge of the front panel, backstitching at the beginning and end of the topstitching seam.

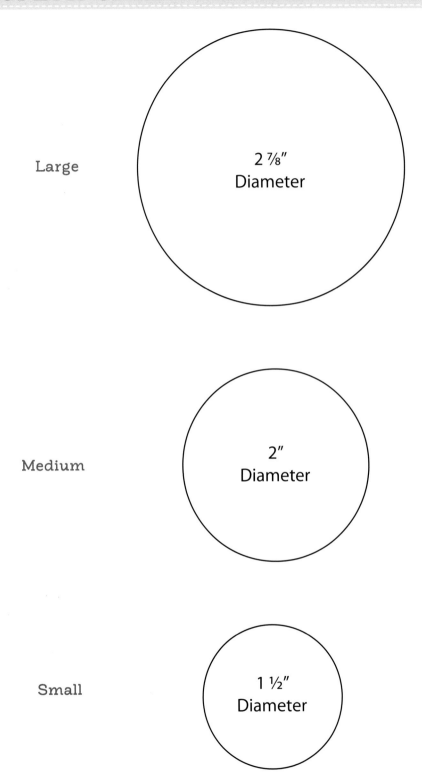

Large

2 ⅞"
Diameter

Medium

2"
Diameter

Small

1 ½"
Diameter

Looking for a great reason to get together? Try hosting a Julia and Julia party! Elissa sent out invitations and prepared some Julia Child's classic French recipes (beef bourguignon and chocolate mousse). The girls arrived wearing retro dresses, aprons and pearls. Everyone looked great and had a good time, and we were amazed at the vintage aprons that were unearthed.

Below, from left to right: Melissa Gross, Elissa Willms, Crystal Skriver, Karissa Anderson, Yidong Han.

Brewed With Taste – tea cozy

 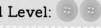
The Duchess of Bedford is attributed to establishing the tradition of Afternoon Tea in the 1840s, and leisurely tea breaks meant teapots sitting for long periods of time while the latest gossip was shared among the aristocracy. Therefore it is no surprise that the first documented tea cozy appeared on the scene in England in 1867.

Although it appears to be a benign little item at the tea table, it does have its own controversy attached to it. The question one must consider is whether to steep the tea with the cozy on or steep the tea and then put the tea cozy on the pot. Advocates of "cozy off" while steeping state that the tea becomes baked if the cozy is left on. "Cozy on" advocates suggest hotter tea for a longer period of time if the cozy is put on once boiling water has been added to the pot.

Whether you are a "cozy on" or "cozy off" advocate, your teapot will be fashion forward in this unique, little tea cozy.

Instructions given are for the black tea cozy.

PROJECT INSPIRATION

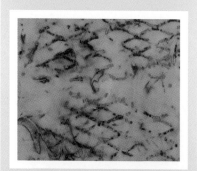

BREWED WITH TASTE – TEA COZY

Materials

- ⅜ yard (.4m) of black tone-on-tone print for outer background
- ⅜ yard (.4m) of black print* for lining
- One fat quarter for bias binding or 90" of prepared bias binding
- 9" × 16" of white for tree appliqué
- Two yards (1.8m) of white yarn for tree appliqué
- Two assorted ¼" buttons in pink and turquoise
- 10 assorted ⅜" buttons in pink and turquoise
- 26 assorted ½" buttons in pink and turquoise
- 12 assorted ⅝" buttons in pink and turquoise
- 16" × 24" of black Soft and Stable (Thermal batting would also work well as it insulates, but it will not create the firm structure that is produced by Soft and Stable.)
- Steam-A-Seam for tree appliqué
- Freezer paper for pattern template
- Fray Check

We suggest using a busy print so that stains and drips do not show on the fabric.

Creating the Outside of the Tea Cozy

1. Trace pattern template onto freezer paper, marking the fold line.

2. Fold black background fabric in half, and iron freezer paper pattern on the fold. Cut out tea cozy background. Repeat for second background piece.

3. Trace two tree pattern pieces onto Steam-A-Seam. Press to the wrong side of the white tree fabric, and cut out two tree appliqués.

4. Center the tree appliqués on each background piece, and press in place. The center of the base of the tree should sit approximately 1 ¾" from the bottom edge of the tea cozy. This will allow room for the row of buttons.

1 ¾"

5. Using white thread, a zigzag stitch and a couching foot on your regular sewing machine, sew the yarn to the tree appliqué. We started at the base of the tree and stitched the yarn to the trunk of the tree and along one of the top branches. Cut the yarn at the tip of the tree branch, but leave a 4" tail of thread to be pulled to the back of the background fabric and tied. Choose another large branch, and sew the yarn to the branch starting at the trunk of the tree and ending at the end of the branch. Again, cut the yarn at the end of the tree branch, and leave a 4" tail of thread to be pulled to the back and knotted. Continue until all of the branches have yarn stitched to them.

6. Pull all white stitching threads to the back of the cozy and tie. Trim ends.

7. Cut the Soft and Stable in half, creating two 12" × 16" pieces. Cut two pieces for lining fabric to match. Sandwich the Soft and Stable between the lining fabric and one outer tea cozy piece, right sides facing out. Pin the outer tea cozy piece in place, and quilt as desired. We quilted swirls in black thread around the tree. Baste a scant ¼" from the outside edge of the tea cozy piece. Trim the Soft and Stable and lining fabric even with the outer edges of the tea cozy piece. Repeat for the second side of the tea cozy.

Putting It All Together

1. Cut the binding fat quarter into 2¼" bias binding strips, and sew together using a 45 degree angle seam to create one continuous binding strip. Bind each piece of the tea cozy separately. Bind each piece as if you were binding a quilt.

2. Arrange half of the buttons on the outside of the tea cozy in an arrangement that you find pleasing. We used 14 assorted pink and turquoise buttons on the tree appliqué and 11 along the bottom of the tea cozy. The bottom row of buttons is a generous ⅛" from the binding edge. Add a dab of Fray Check to the thread used to sew each button in place to further secure the buttons.

⅛"

3. If you would like an opening in each side of the tea cozy for the handle and the spout, lay the tea cozy template on top of the cozy pieces and mark the openings with a pin or a chalk pencil.

Hopscotch Hint: *Many tea cozies have a loop at the top. If you would like to add a loop, mark the top middle of the tea cozy with a pin or marking tool. Cut a 4" piece of prepared bias binding from the remaining binding strip. Fold in half along the length of the strip, matching the two folded edges. Topstitch the folds together, sewing ⅛" from the folded edge. Fold the bias binding piece in half, with raw edges together, to form a loop. Place the loop on the inside of one tea cozy piece, and baste to the top middle of the piece. The raw edges are facing the inside of the tea cozy, and the loop is facing away from the cozy. Proceed with step 4.*

4. Lay the two tea cozy pieces on top of one another, wrong sides together, and pin. Using a needle and coordinating color of thread, slip stitch the two pieces together. If you have marked an opening for the teapot handle and spout (step 3), start and stop your stitching line to allow for each opening. If you have added a loop at the top of the tea cozy, be sure to stitch through the loop when sewing the two sides of the tea cozy together. Remove basting stitching from the loop if required.

Rusting Fabric

The fall version of the tea cozy is made using rusted fabric. We love the look of rusting and find rusted fabric simple to prepare. Be sure to wear old clothes when rusting as it can stain.

1. To rust fabric, begin with plain cream or white cotton fabric. We cut our fabric into 20" × 20" or 20" × 40" pieces before rusting.

2. Source out fabulous pieces of rusted metal — the more interesting the shape, the better. We find that smaller pieces of metal like nails, washers and screws work better than large pieces. Welders and farmers can be excellent sources of interesting pieces of rusted metal. Heather found some of our pieces by walking along the railroad tracks and picking up metal ties and hooks that had been cast aside by railway workers.

3. Pour a few inches of white vinegar into a bowl, and dip the fabric into the vinegar to wet it thoroughly.

4. Wrap the metal pieces in the fabric, and place in a black trash bag. Leave to sit 24 hours.

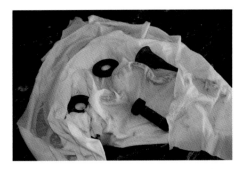

"Never trust a man who, when left alone in a room with a tea cosy, does not try it on."
— Billy Connolly

5. After 24 hours, unwrap the fabric, and rinse in the sink. Wash in the washing machine with a mild soap, and dry in the dryer. If you would like your fabric to be rustier, simply repeat the process.

We do not recommend leaving the fabric to rust longer than 24 hours as it can rust right through the cotton and leave holes. Of course if that is the look you want, leave the fabric in the bag for a longer period of time. You can keep checking the fabric to see how the process is coming along.

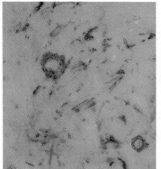 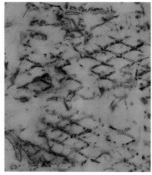

TRY AN ALTERNATE COLORWAY

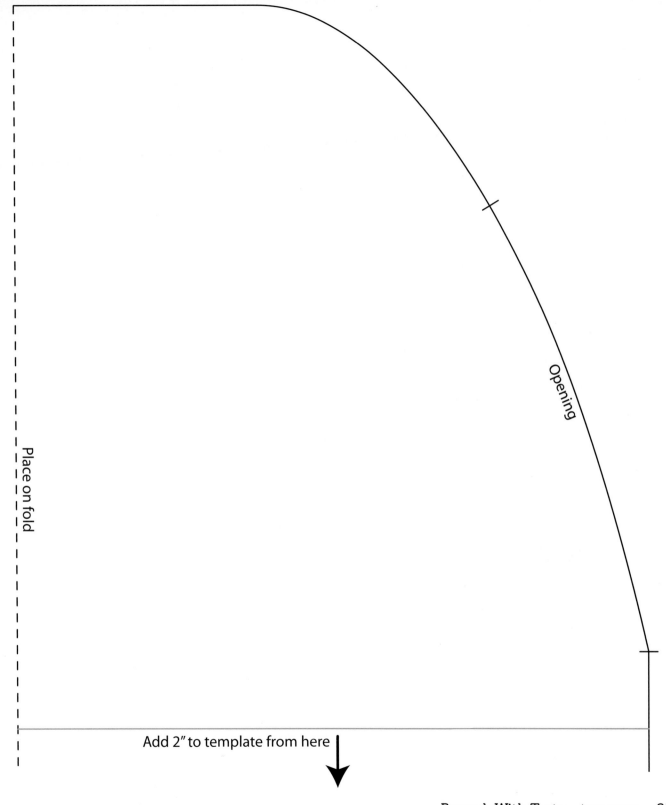

Place on fold

Opening

Add 2" to template from here

Garden Grace — table runner

Tidy up the scrap bin, and create an awesome table runner at the same time! Delightful embroidered circles bring the garden to the table.

Instructions given are for the blue/lime green version of the table runner.

PROJECT INSPIRATION

Materials

- ¾ yard (.7m) of assorted blue prints. The more prints the better.
- ⅛ yard (.2m) of solid lime green for circle appliqués
- ¼ yard (.25m) of solid blue for binding
- 20" × 37" of batting
- ⅝ yards (.6m) of blue print for backing
- #12 pearle cotton in assorted blue and purple tones
- Freezer paper or Steam-A-Seam (depending on appliqué method chosen)

Cutting

From assorted blue prints, cut:
6 — 3½" × 6½" rectangles
12 — 2" × 10½" rectangles
7 — 2½" × 16½" rectangles

From solid blue for binding, cut:
3 — 2¼" × width of fabric

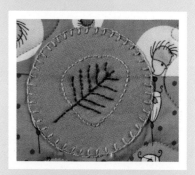

Piecing the Runner Top

1. Sew two 2" × 10½" rectangles together along the 10½" side. Press seam toward the darkest print. Repeat with the remaining 2" × 10½" rectangles for a total of 6 units.

Make 6

2. Sew a 3½" × 6½" rectangle to the end of each unit created in step one. Press seam toward the 3½" × 6½" rectangle. Repeat with the remaining 5 units.

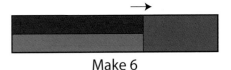

Make 6

3. Sew the runner top together following the layout diagram below.

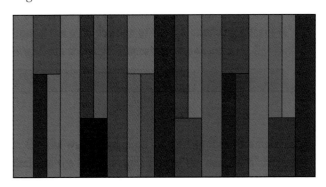

Embroidered Motifs:

Appliqué using Freezer Paper
The blue runner uses needle turn appliqué to attach the embroidered circles.

1. Using a light box (or window) and mechanical pencil, trace the embroidery motifs onto the solid lime green background fabric. Be sure to leave 3" between motifs to allow enough room for the circle appliqué. Center your embroidery along the width of the yardage.

2. Embroider the motifs using a backstitch and #12 pearle cotton in an assortment of blue and purple tones. Use French knots for the flower centers and the end of the bird's tail feathers.

3. Trace 6 circles onto the smooth side of the freezer paper. Cut circles out on the trace lines. Place the motifs back on the light box, and center a freezer paper circle on top of an embroidery motif. Iron in place (not on the light box!). Trim the circle to within a scant ¼" of the freezer paper. Repeat for the remaining five motifs.

4. Lay the six circles on the runner top, and find an arrangement that you find pleasing. Appliqué in place.

Appliqué using Steam-A-Seam

The circles on the gray and pastel tone runner are appliquéd using Steam-A-Seam.

1. Trace six circles onto the smooth side of the Steam-A-Seam. Cut out the circles ¼" larger than the trace line.

2. Appliqué the motifs onto the solid fabric. Be sure to leave 3" between motifs to allow enough room for the circle appliqué. Center your embroidery along the width of the yardage. Once all six motifs have been appliquéd, turn the fabric wrong side up. Center the Steam-A-Seam circles over the appliqué motifs. You will be able to see through the Steam-A-Seam, and therefore can center it perfectly. Iron in place.

3. Trim circles along the trace line, and remove the paper. Lay the six circles on the runner top, and find an arrangement that you find pleasing. Press in place.

4. Using a button-hole stitch and #8 gray pearle cotton, stitch around each circle.

Putting It All Together

1. Layer batting between the runner top and backing with the right sides facing out. Pin in place. Quilt as desired. We quilted an all-over loop pattern on our runner (we do not have any quilting on the embroidered circles).

2. Trim runner to ⅛" from the edge of the runner top so that a little of the batting is showing. This will create a full and solid binding edge once the binding has been sewn in place.

3. Sew the 2¼"-wide binding strips end to end, using a 45 degree seam, to create one continuous binding strip. Fold the binding strip in half, wrong sides together, along the length of the strip. Press.

4. Bind runner.

TRY AN ALTERNATE COLORWAY

Traveling Java — coffee cup wrap

Finished Size: 3 ½" × 11"   Skill Level:

Coffee is embedded into life at the Willms. These awesome little wraps will fit an assortment of disposable cups and add bling to coffee on the go. Try rusting your own fabric for an antique touch (instructions for rusting can be found on page 22).

Heather is totally addicted to making these!

Instructions are for the tree wrap.

Materials for Basic Wrap

- 6" × 14" of two different green prints for front and back
- 6" × 14" lightweight batting*
- ¾" × 1 ½" sewable hook and loop Velcro**
- Freezer paper

This is not the time to use a sturdy batting or a thermo batting, as it is too heavy and will make construction of the wrap difficult. We used Hobbs 80/20 batting for our wraps.

**To add style to your wrap, check out the amazing assortment of colored Velcro on the market.*

Tree:

- 5" × 5" black cotton for appliquéd circle
- 3" × 3" green wool for leaf appliqué
- Rust-colored 3-strand variegated floss for embroidery
- 10 small rust beads
- Two rust ½" buttons for the outer edge of the wrap

Bird:

- 5" × 5" red cotton for appliquéd circle
- 3" × 3" blue cotton for bird appliqué
- #12 yellow pearle cotton for embroidery for beak and feet
- #12 teal pearle cotton for tail appliqué,
- Three yellow beads for tail
- ¼" brown button for eye
- Two teal ½" buttons for the outer edge of the wrap

Flower:

- 5" × 5" brown dot cotton for appliquéd circle
- 2" × 2" green wool
- 2" × 2" of pink wool for flower appliqué
- #12 green and white pearle cotton
- Three white seed beads
- Two ½" green buttons for outer edge of the wrap

Creating the Wrap

1. Trace wrap pattern template and circle pattern template onto the smooth side of freezer paper. Cut out on the traced line.

2. With the shiny side of the freezer paper touching the fabric, iron the wrap template onto the **right** side of the green print for the front of the wrap, and cut out the template. Remove template. Now, iron the wrap template onto the **wrong** side of the green print for the back of the wrap, and cut out the template. Be sure to use the shiny side of the freezer paper to iron on the fabric.

3. Iron the freezer paper template onto batting and cut out. Using a ruler and rotary cutter, trim ¼" off of each end of the batting piece. This will ease turning and sewing up the open end of the wrap once it is turned.

4. Lay the front and back wrap pieces right sides together on top of the batting, and pin in place. Check that the three pieces are aligned. Stitch around the wrap using a ¼" seam, leaving the indicated end open for turning.

5. Using a pair of scissors, trim the seam allowance around the wrap to a scant ¼" (or a generous ⅛"). Notch outside curved seams, and clip inside curved seams. Clip the corners at each edge of the circle as indicated below.

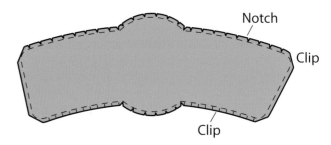

6. Turn wrap right side out and press. Turn the raw edges of the open end into the wrap, pin and hand stitch closed using a slip stitch.

7. Topstitch around the wrap ¼" from the edge, and quilt parallel lines along the width of the wrap. Backstitch the beginning and end of each quilting line. This will create a sturdy wrap surface.

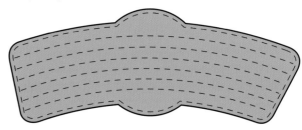

8. Appliqué the motif of your choice onto the 5" × 5" circle fabric. For appliqué options and instructions, see page 37. Embroider details on the motif but do not add buttons or beads at this point.

9. Using a light box or window, center the freezer paper circle template on top of the appliqué, using the top and bottom marks to ensure that the motif is upright. Press in place with an iron. **Not on the light box! Move it to the ironing board first.** Trim away excess fabric around the circle so that a scant ¼" is showing beyond the freezer paper.

10. Pin the circle onto the wrap, ensuring that the top and bottom of the freezer paper circle are aligned with the top and bottom of the wrap. Appliqué in place. Remove freezer paper template.

11. Sew on any buttons and beads in the circle motif. Using a contrasting color of #12 pearle cotton, stitch a running stitch approximately ⅛" inside the edge of the circle.

12. Using a coordinating color of Velcro, place the soft loop side of the Velcro rectangle **under** the right edge of the wrap. Align the long edge of the Velcro with the outside right edge of the wrap, leaving ⅛" between the Velcro and the edge of the wrap. Stitch in place. We stitched around the edge of the Velcro rectangle, backstitching at the beginning and end of our stitching line.

13. Sew the coarse hook side of the Velcro onto the **top** left side of the wrap, again aligning the long side of the Velcro rectangle with the outside edge of the wrap, leaving ⅛" between the edge of the Velcro and the edge of the wrap.

14. Sew decorative buttons onto the right edge of the wrap. They are a bit tricky to sew, as it is difficult to sew through the Velcro beneath. If the Velcro is too thick, sew the buttons on by stitching them to the top layer of the wrap, rather than trying to go through all of the layers.

Hopscotch Hint: *For a perfect gift, tuck a gift card into a closed coffee wrap!*

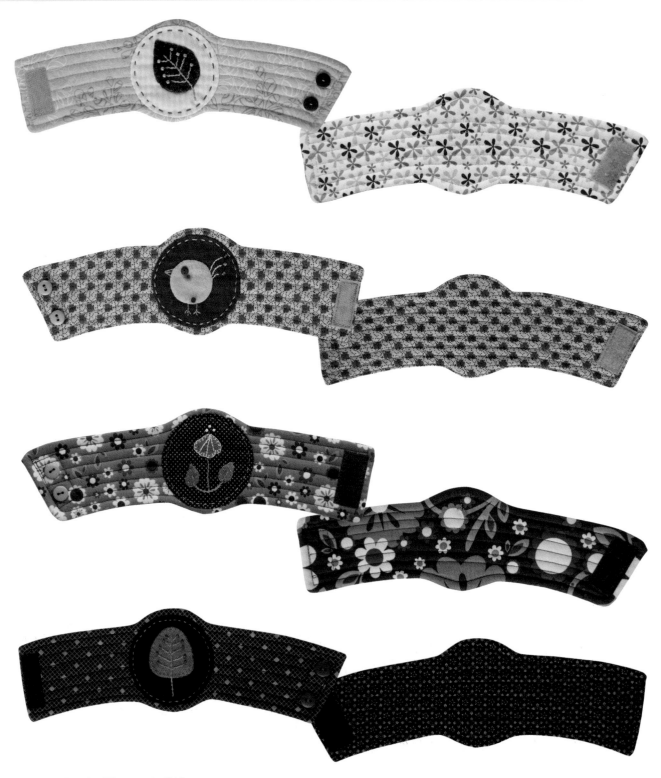

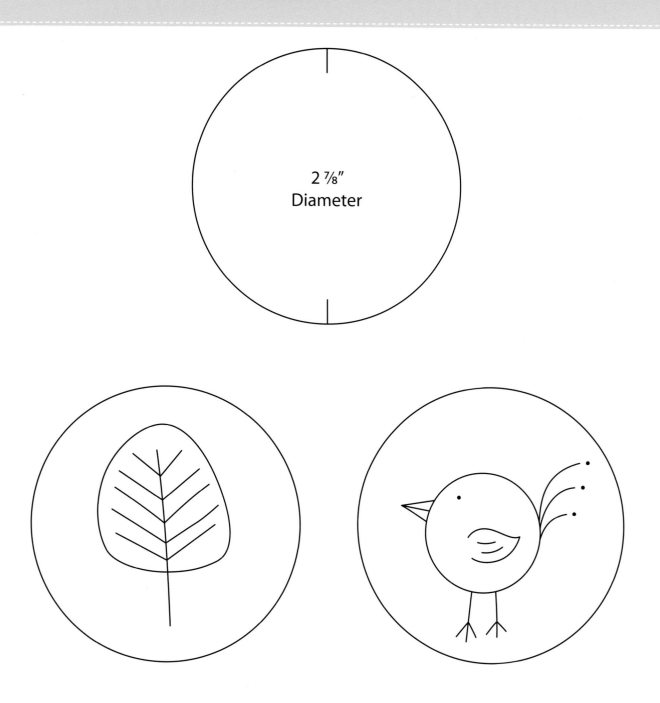

2 ⅞"
Diameter

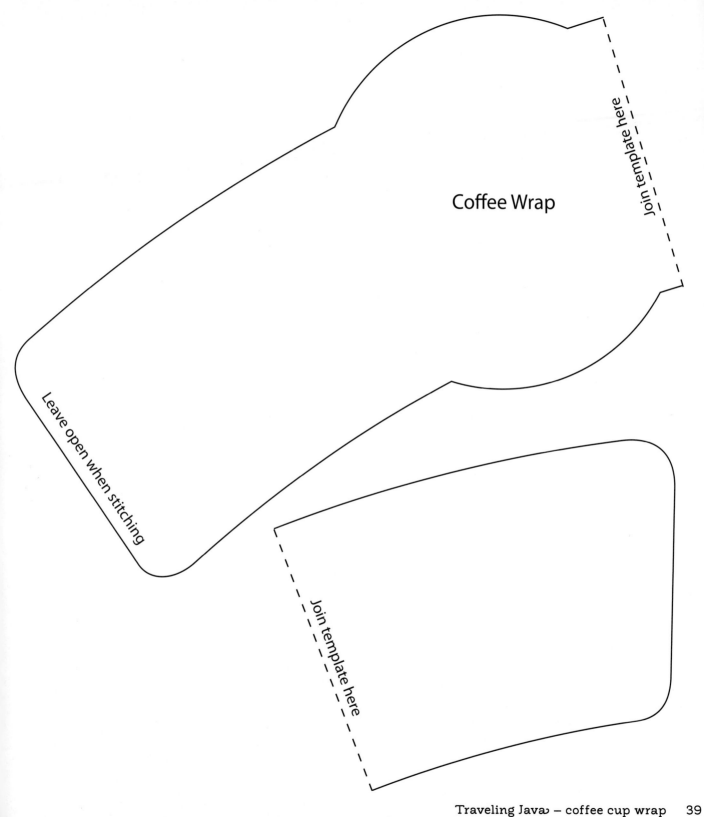

Coffee Wrap

Join template here

Leave open when stitching

Join template here

Trendy Tea Towels

Add a touch of style to your everyday tea towels by appliquéing a bit of color to each one. These quick and easy gifts add whimsy to your kitchen or the homes of friends and family.

Materials

Bee Towel:

- One turquoise tea towel (approx. 20" × 28")
- 3" × 8" white print for wings
- 3" × 7" black for stripes
- 3" × 9" yellow print for bee bodies
- #12 pearle cotton for appliqué
- Nine black beads
- Steam-A-Seam

Circle Towel:

- One red striped tea towel (approx. 20" × 28")
- 4" × 4" cream floral print
- 5" × 8" black floral print
- One ¾", one ½" and one ¼" red button
- Steam-A-Seam

Flower Towel:

- One pink tea towel (approx. 20" × 28")
- Three 4" × 4" squares of floral prints
- Three ¾" purple buttons
- Steam-A-Seam

PROJECT INSPIRATION

Creating the Tea Towel

1. Prewash the tea towel before appliquéing shapes to remove sizing and any chemical finishes on the tea towel.

2. Trace the appliqué shapes onto the smooth side of Steam-A-Seam.

Bee: Trace three of each shape. For the wings of the bee, add a scant ¼" along the lower edge of the wings, as this will be tucked under the bee when ironing the bee to the tea towel.

Circles: Trace the three circles.

Flower: Trace three circles and draw three ½" wide stems that are 9", 6" and 3" long.

3. Cut out shapes ¼" beyond the trace line.

4. Iron the shapes to the back of the corresponding fabric. Cut out the shapes on the trace line.

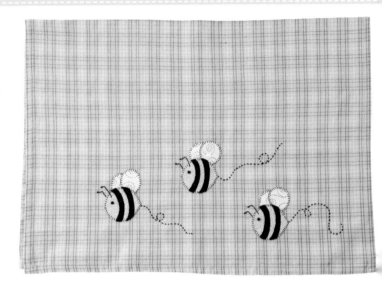

5. Position the shapes on the tea towels. For the bee, tuck a scant ¼" of the bottom edge of the wings under the body of the bee. Press in place.

6. Stitch the pieces in place using black thread (we used purple for the flower tea towel) and a machine blanket stitch. Secure the start and end of stitching by putting a dab of Fray Check on the stitching.

7. Add stitching and embroidery.

Bees: With a pencil, draw the antenna and a flight swirl behind each bee. With #12 black pearle cotton, use a stem stitch to embroider the antennas and a running stitch to embroider a flight swirl behind each bee. Sew a black bead to each bee for the eyes and a bead to the end of each antenna.

Circles: Sew a red button to each circle. The three sizes of buttons correspond with the three sizes of circles.

Flowers: Sew a button to each flower.

8. Secure all buttons and beads with Fray Check.

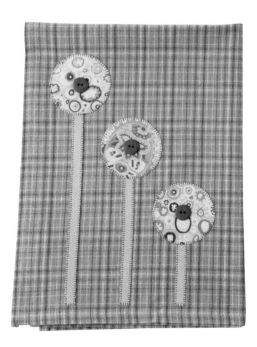

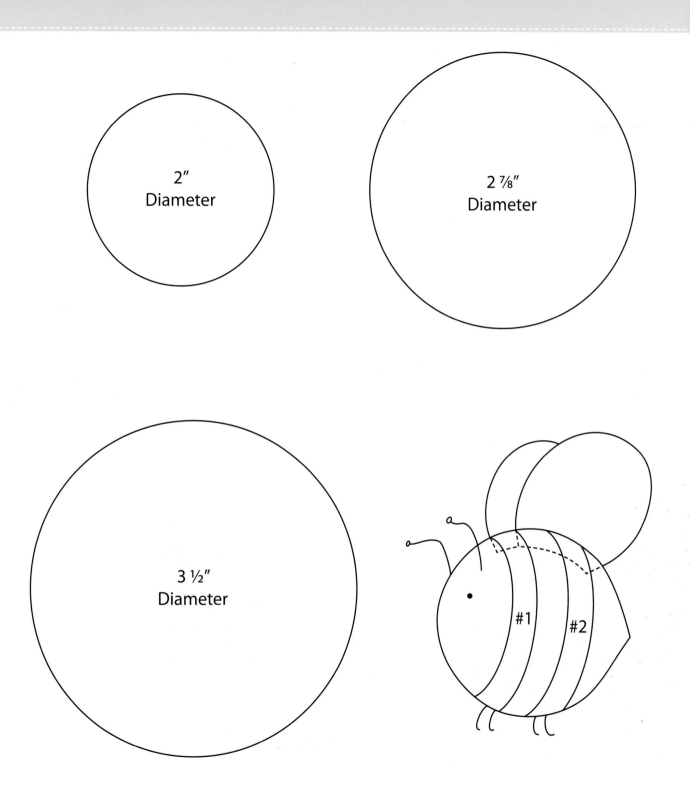

2″
Diameter

2 ⅞″
Diameter

3 ½″
Diameter

#1 #2

Lunch To Go – lunch bag

Finished Size: 6" H × 9½" L × 6" W

Skill Level:

Arrive at work or school with the unique and fashionable lunch bag of them all. Besides carrying lunch, this tote is perfect for packing projects, tools and your favorite ephemera. Use leftover fabric to create a matching napkin!

Materials and instructions are for the turquoise geometric bag.

Materials

- ⅝ yd (.6m) of heavy weight geometric print for outside of bag
- ⅝ yd (.6m) of turquoise stripe for lining
- ¼ yd (.2m) of turquoise dot for handle and button tabs
- 25" × 32" of Soft and Stable or any firm batting
- Two 1" buttons
- Two ⅞" (size 10–21mm) snaps
- Freezer paper for pattern templates

Cutting

From heavy weight cotton for outside of bag, cut:
1 — 7" × 28" for side of bag
1 — 11½" × 16½" for top and bottom
1 — 2" × 22½" for rim of top
1 — 2" × 6" for back tab

From turquoise stripe for lining, cut:
1 — 6" × 26½" for side of bag
1 — 10½" × 15" for top and bottom
1 — 2" × 22½" for rim of top
1 — 2" × 6" for back tab

From turquoise dot for handle and button tabs, cut:
2 — 2" × 7½" for handle
4 — 2" × 4" for button tabs

From Soft and Stable, cut:
1 — 7" × 28" for body
1 — 11½" × 16½" for top and bottom
1 — 1¾" × 22¼" for rim of top
1 — 1¾" × 5¾" for back tab
1 — 1¾" × 7¼" for handle
2 — 1¾" × 3¾" for button tabs

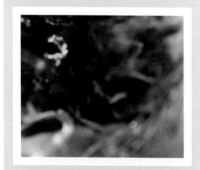

Creating the Bottom of the Bag

We recommend you layer and quilt the fabric for the sides, top and bottom before cutting out the bag templates. If you cut out the templates and then layer and quilt them, the quilting could change the size of the finished pieces. Step 1 provides instructions for layering and quilting before moving on to instructions for cutting out the templates.

1. With right sides facing up, place the 7" × 28" and 11½" × 16½" pieces of outside fabric on top of the corresponding-sized pieces of Soft and Stable. Quilt as desired. We quilted curving lines along the length of the side piece and across the length of the top and bottom of the bag.

2. Trace the bag top and bottom template onto freezer paper, transferring all markings. Iron both pieces to the 11½" × 16½" quilted piece created in step one. Cut out a top and bottom piece. Transfer markings onto the quilted pieces with your favorite marking tool.

3. From the 7" × 28" quilted piece from step one, cut a 5½" × 26½" rectangle for the side of the bag.

4. Fold the 5½" × 26½" in half, right sides together, so that the 5½" sides are aligned. Sew a seam along the 5½" sides to create a loop. Backstitch at the beginning and end of the seam. Press with seam allowance open.

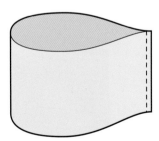

5. Fold the loop in half, right sides together, and mark the opposite side of the seam with a pin. Fold the loop again, matching the seam and the pin you have just used to mark half of the bag. Mark the folds again with pins. You should now have 3 marks and a seam line to divide the bag into 4 equal sections. This will help when sewing the bag sides to the bottom.

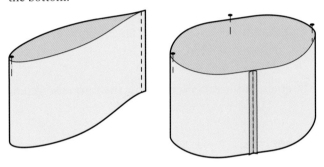

6. Pin the bag side loop to the quilted bottom, matching pins to markings on the quilted bottom. Match the seam of the loop with a mark on the long side of the bag base. This will put the seam at the back of the finished bag. Pin at the markings, and ease the remaining edges in place. Sew around the base of the bag beginning and ending with a backstitch. Turn right side out and finger press.

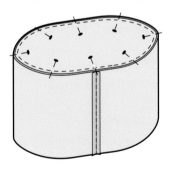

7. Iron freezer paper templates for the top and bottom of the bag onto the 10½" × 15" rectangle of lining fabric. Cut out and transfer all markings to the lining fabric. Repeat steps 4-6 with the lining.

8. Turn quilted exterior of the bag wrong side out so that the Soft and Stable is on the outside. The lining should be right side out for this step. Mark the quarter of the bag along the top edge of each piece in the same way we marked the bottom in steps 4 and 5.

9. Place the lining inside of the bag and pin the two pieces together along the top of the bag, matching all pin markings and the back seams. Sew a ¼" seam around the top of the bag, leaving a 3½" opening along the back of the bag for turning.

10. Turn the bag right side out through the opening. Tuck the lining into the bag. Fold the lining over the outside edge of the bag so that a ½" of the lining is exposed. Hand sew the opening used for turning closed using a slip stitch.

11. Check to be sure that a ½" of lining is exposed around the outside rim of the bag. Topstitch along the edge of the lining, stitching along the lower edge of the exposed lining (closest to the outside fabric).

Creating the Top of the Bag

1. To create the rim of the top of the bag, place the 2" × 22½" of outside fabric on top of the 2" × 22½" lining fabric, right sides together. Center the 1¾" × 22¼" rectangle of Soft and Stable on top of these two fabrics. Sew along both 2" sides, backstitching at the beginning and end of each seam. Sew along one 22½" side, backstitching at the beginning and end of the seam. Clip corners, and turn right side out. Sew the raw edges of the open side together using a basting stitch and sewing a scant ¼" from the outside edge.

2. Topstitch along the sides and bottom of the rim, leaving the top of the rim basted.

Baste

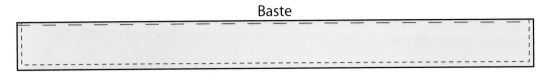

3. Repeat steps 1–2 with the 2" × 6" outside fabric and lining and the 1¾" × 5¾" Soft and Stable to create the back tab.

4. Repeat steps 1–2 again using the four 2" × 4" rectangles of accent fabric and the two 1¾" × 3¾" rectangles of Soft and Stable to create the button tabs. You will be using two 2" × 4" of accent fabric and one 1¾" × 3¾" rectangle of Soft and Stable to create each button tab. When sewing the tabs, sew along the 4" sides and the 2" bottom, leaving the 2" top side open for turning. Repeat for a second button tab.

Make 2

5. To create the handle, place the two 2" × 7½" rectangles of accent fabric right sides together. Center the 1¾" × 7¼" of Soft and Stable on top of these two pieces. Stitch around the rectangle, leaving a 3" opening for turning. Clip corners.

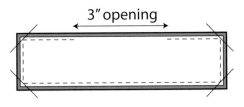

3" opening

6. Turn and press. Hand sew the opening closed using a slip stitch. Topstitch around the outside edge of the handle, stitching ⅛" from the edge.

7. Center the handle to the quilted bag top, placing the ends of the handle 2" from each side of the top. Pin in place. Stitch the handle to the quilted top, stitching a 1¼" × ½" rectangle on each end of the handle.

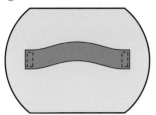

8. Center the back tab along one side of the quilted bag top, matching the center of the back tab with the center marking on the quilted top. The outer fabric of the tab is next to the quilted bag top, and the lining side is facing up. Pin in place. Place the button tabs on the opposite side of the bag top, positioning the outside of each button tab a ½" from the outside corner.

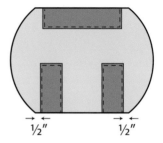

9. Baste around the edge of the quilted top, using a scant ¼" seam. Be sure to baste through all thicknesses when basting the back tab and button tabs in place.

LUNCH TO GO – LUNCH BAG

TRY AN ALTERNATE COLORWAY

10. Mark the center of the bag top rim piece with a pin, marking on the basted edge. Match the center of the bag top rim with the mark between the button tabs on the quilted top. Pin in place. Pin each outer edge of the rim piece ⅛" from the back tab. Pin the remaining edge of the rim piece to the outer edge of the quilted bag top, easing the rim in place. Stitch in place using a scant ¼" seam. Backstitch at the beginning and end of the stitching line.

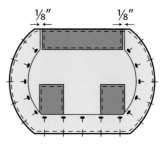

11. Place the bag top lining on top of the quilted bag top, right sides together. Pin in place. Using a ¼" seam, sew around the top of the bag, starting halfway through one button tab and stopping halfway through the second tab. The space between the two button tabs should be left open for turning.

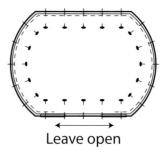

Leave open

12. Turn the bag top right side out, and finger press everything in place. Hand sew the opening at the front of the quilted top closed using a slip stitch. The bag top is now complete.

13. Sew the button tabs to the rim of the bag top by topstitching along the outer edge of the bag rim, sewing across the button tabs. This stitching line should line up with the topstitching already in place on the outer edge of the rim.

Putting It All Together

1. Pin the back tab of the lid to the bottom section of the bag, centering the middle of the back tab with the seam on the side of the bottom section. We left ⅛" between the bag top and the bag bottom section.

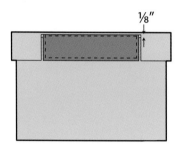

2. Stitch the lid to the bag by topstitching around the back tab, ⅛" from the edge of the tab. See stitching line on diagram in step 1.

3. Sew buttons to the button tabs, placing them ¼" from the bottom edge of the tab and centering the button on the width of the tab.

4. Sew one-half of the snap to the underside of the button tab. Center the snap in the same position as the button on the reverse side of the tab. Repeat for the second tab.

TRY AN ALTERNATE COLORWAY

5. Close the bag to find the placement of the second half of each snap. We found it helpful to fill the bag with extra batting when measuring for the second half of the snap. This ensures that the bag is it's true shape and size. Measure down 1" from the edge of the exposed lining, and sew the second half of the snap in place. The two snaps that are sewn to the bag should be 4" apart, from center of snap to center of snap.

6. If you would like to further secure the back corners of the bag top rim, sew a 1" × 1" square of Velcro onto the underside of each corner. Attach the corresponding 1" × 1" piece of Velcro to the side of the bag.

Hopscotch Hint: *We used laminate for the lining of the green and orange lunch bag. While it is a bit trickier to sew, it creates a washable liner, perfect for spills and condensation from cool lunch items. When sewing with laminate, try using a Teflon sewing machine foot that is designed for use with hard to handle fabrics (i.e., suede, leather and vinyl) which may stick to the sewing machine foot.*

Hopscotch Hint: *Eating a packed lunch is certainly not the highlight of Heather's school day. Preparing and packing a salad the night before school can be a challenge to manage, but a salad in a jar makes the perfect alternative to the packed sandwich. Pack the jars on the weekend, making sure that the dressing and moister ingredients are at the bottom of the jar and the greens are at the top. Store the jars in the refrigerator until needed. Shake the jar or empty the contents of the jar onto a plate before eating.*

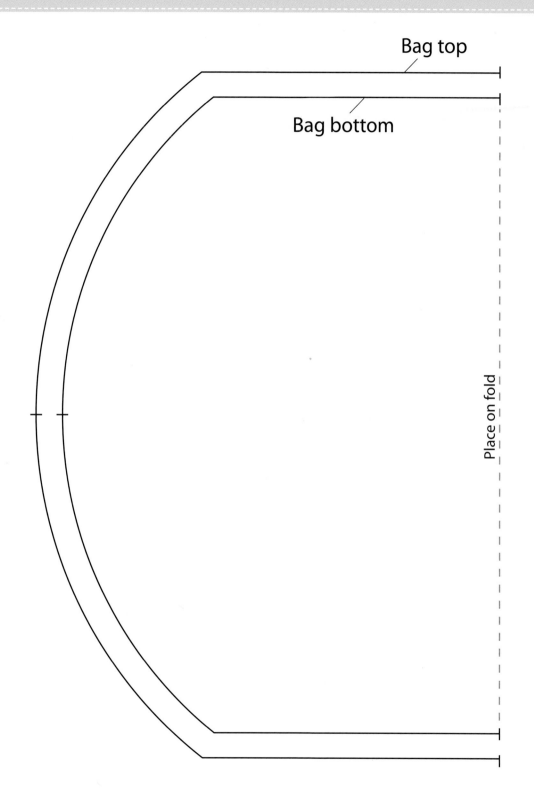

Bag top

Bag bottom

Place on fold

Savour the Garden – placemat

A touch of embroidery makes these placemats a treat to make and use. They are the perfect gift for the flower gardener or the friend who has everything. Customize the placemats by choosing the perfect prints and color combination for that special someone (or yourself).

Materials and instructions are for the spring print version of the placemats.

Materials for two placemats:

- ⅝ yd (.6m) total of assorted spring prints for placemat tops
- ⅛ yd (.1m) of solid gray for stitching background
- ⅓ yd (.3m) of green for binding
- ⅝ yd (.6m) of backing print
- Assorted #12 pearle cotton in colors that coordinate with the spring prints for embroidery

Cutting instructions are for ONE placemat.

The placemat is pieced in rows. Measurements are given for each row. You may choose to use 13 prints for the 13 rows or repeat some of the prints in two or more rows. Refer to the piecing diagram when cutting out the placemat rows.

From assorted prints, cut:
Row 1 — 1½" × 14½"
Row 2 — 2" × 11½" and 1½" × 2"
Row 3 — 1½" × 4" and 1½" × 8"
Row 4 — 2" × 14½"
Row 5 — 2½" × 7½" and 2½" × 6"
Row 6 — 1½" × 2" and 1½" × 11½"
Row 7 — 1½" × 10½" and 1½" × 2"
Row 8 — 2½" × 14½"
Row 9 — 1½" × 4½" and 1½" × 8"
Row 10 — 2" × 13"
Row 11 — 1½" × 14½"
Row 12 — 2½" × 7" and 2½" × 6"
Row 13 — 2" × 13½"

PROJECT INSPIRATION

From the gray solid, cut the following for **ONE** placemat:
1 — 2½" × width of fabric
1 — 1½" × width of fabric

From the 2½" strip, cut:
2 — 2" × 2½" (Rows 2 and 5)
1 — 2" × 2" (Row 10)
1 — 2½" × 2½" (Row 12)

From the 1½" strip, cut:
1 — 1½" × 3½" (Row 3)
2 — 1½" × 2" (Rows 6 and 13)
2 — 1½" × 3" (Rows 7 and 9)

Use the remainder of each strip to cut the pieces for the second placemat.

From green binding fabric, cut:
2 — 2¼" × width of fabric

From backing print and batting, cut:
Batting — 17½" × 21½"
Backing — 17½" × 21½"

Assembling the Placemat Top

1. Assemble the placemat top following the layout diagram below. Sew the pieces into rows where required, pressing all seams away from the gray blocks. Sew the rows together to create the top, again pressing seams away from the rows containing gray blocks wherever possible.

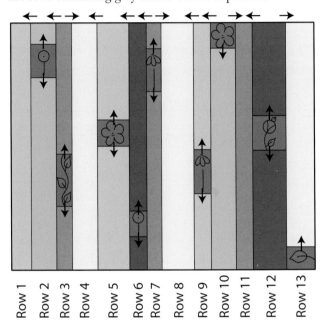

2. Secure the edges of the placemat by stay stitching around the outside of the placemat a scant ¼" from the edge. Press.

3. Using a light box and a mechanical pencil, trace the stitched motifs on page 59 onto the appropriate gray blocks. Refer to the layout diagram above as needed.

4. Using a backstitch and an assortment of coordinating threads, embroider the motifs onto the placemat. We used #12 pearle cotton to embroider our placemats.

Putting It All Together

1. Layer batting between the placemat top and backing, with the right sides facing out. Pin in place. Quilt as desired. We quilted an all-over loop pattern on our placemats (we did not quilt on the embroidered gray blocks).

2. Trim placemats to an ⅛" from the edge of the placemat top so that a little of the batting is showing. This will create a full and solid binding edge once the binding has been sewn in place.

3. Sew the 2¼"-wide binding strips end to end, using a 45 degree diagonal seam, to create one continuous binding strip. Fold the binding strip in half, wrong sides together, along the length of the strip. Press.

4. Bind placemats.

Repeat to create the second placemat.

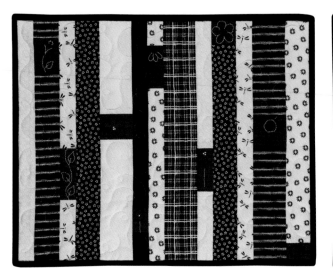
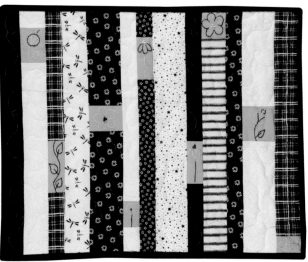
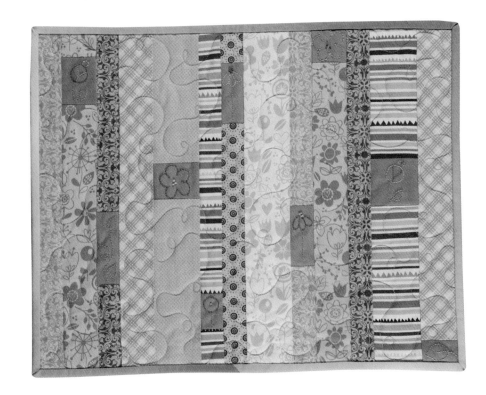

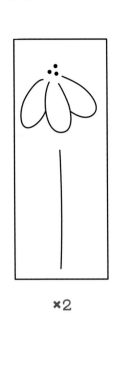

×2

×2

×2

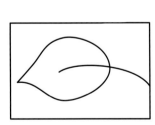

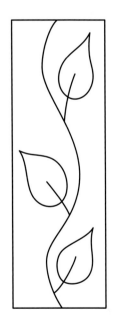

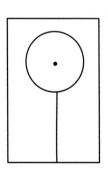

Bubbly Chic — wine bottle bag

While traveling in Japan several years ago, we went prepared with gifts for the people we visited. After a school visit in Toyota city, we thanked the principal of the school by giving him a bottle of Canadian maple syrup. There was an awkward pause as we thanked him and presented him with the syrup. After the visit, we asked our friend who was living in Japan what had gone wrong. He explained that in Japan, you never offer a "naked" gift. Our bottle of maple syrup should have been wrapped or in a gift bag!

Don't make the same mistake with your next gift of wine. Whether for a hostess gift or a birthday present, dress your wine bottle for the occasion. Just make sure it is not dressed better than you are! This gift bag fits a standard 750mL wine bottle.

PROJECT INSPIRATION

Materials

Basic bottle bag:
- 11½" × 11½" for bottom of bag
- 11½" × 20½" for lining and bag top
- 27" of ⅝"-wide grosgrain ribbon
- ⅝" button
- Fray Check
- Freezer paper or Steam-A-Seam

Black and white bag:
- 2½" × 11½" black-and-white stripe for front panel
- Two 5" × 11½" rectangles of black dot for side panels
- 11½" × 20½" white scribble for lining and bag top
- One ⅝" white button
- Six ½" red buttons
- 27" of ⅝" black grosgrain ribbon.

Brown and orange bag:

- Four 1½" × 3½", two 2" × 3½" and two 2½ × 3½" rectangles of assorted cream, yellow and green prints
- Two 6" × 11½" orange rectangles for side panels
- 11½" × 20½" brown print for lining and bag top
- Six ¼" – ¾" assorted brown buttons
- 27" of ½" cream twill tape.

Turquoise and red bag:

- 3" × 11½" light blue for front panel
- Two 4¾" × 11½" rectangles of turquoise print for side panels
- 11½" × 20½" blue polka dot for lining and bag top
- 3" × 3" square of red wool
- 2" × 3" of green wool
- Three ¼" red buttons for flower
- One ⅝" turquoise button
- Green and red #8 pearle cotton
- 27" of ½" red ribbon

The construction of the bag is the same for all of the bags we have created. The bottom of the bag is made from an 11½" square, and what you do with that square determines the design of the bag. We have included instructions for the 11½" square in the three bags we created, but once you get started, there is no end to the possibilities! Just remember not to sew any embellishments to the bottom 2" of the 11½" square, as that part of the bag will sit under the base of the wine bottle.

Creating the Front Panel

Black and white bag:

1. Sew the 2½" × 11½" black-and-white-striped rectangle in between the two 5" × 11½" black dot rectangles, sewing along the 11½" sides. Press seams away from the center panel.

2. Sew the six ½" red buttons down the front of the bag. Start 1" from the top of the panel, and space the buttons evenly down the panel. The last button should be sewn 2½" from the bottom, as the bottom portion of the panel will sit under the base of the bottle when the bag contains a bottle of wine.

Construct the bag following the "Bag Construction" instructions on page 65.

Brown and orange bag:

1. Lay the assorted 1½" × 3½", 2" × 3½" and 2½ × 3½" cream, yellow and green rectangles in a row, and find an arrangement that you find pleasing. Sew the rectangles together along the 3½" sides to form a panel. Press seams in one direction.

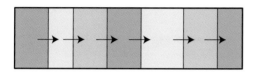

2. The curved piecing on the front panel is done by free curve piecing. If this technique is new for you, practice with several strips of scrap fabric until you feel confident with the process.

On the cutting mat, lay a 6" × 11½" orange rectangle beside the pieced front panel with the 11½" sides touching. Both pieces should be right sides up. Pull the orange rectangle on top of the front panel, overlapping the pieces by approximately 1".

Using your rotary cutter, but without a ruler, cut a slightly wavy line through the overlapping fabric. Caution: If your waves are deep, you will have more difficulty sewing the pieces together. We recommend a **gentle** wavy cut.

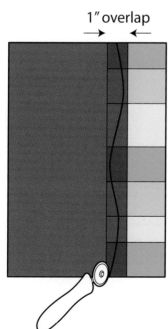

1" overlap

3. Lay the pieces right sides together and pin. The curves will seem awkward, as they appear not to fit when you pin them. Gently align the raw edges, and pin every 2"-3", being careful not to stretch the raw edges, as there will be sections that are on the bias. Stitch along the curved edges using a ¼" seam. Gently press seams toward the orange print.

4. Repeat with the second 6" × 11½" orange rectangle on the opposite side of the panel.

5. Trim the bag bottom to 11½" × 11½" making sure that the pieced panel remains in the center of the square.

6. Sew a button to each of the green and yellow rectangles on the front panel (5 in total). Do not sew a button on the very bottom rectangle. The remaining ⅝" brown button is for securing the ribbon.

Construct the bag following the "Bag Construction" instructions on page 65.

Turquoise and red bag:

1. Sew the 3" × 11½" turquoise rectangle in between the two 4¾" × 11½" turquoise print rectangles, sewing along the 11½" sides. Press seams away from the center panel.

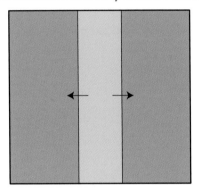

2. Trace one flower and two leaf motifs (found on page 66) onto freezer paper. Cut out motifs on the traced lines. Iron the flower template onto the red wool and the leaves onto the green wool. Cut out motifs, and remove freezer paper.

3. Pin the flower motif onto the center panel, placing it 2½" from the top of the panel. Using a mechanical pencil, draw a line down the center of the panel. Start the pencil line at the base of the flower, and continue down to the bottom of the panel. The line does not have to be straight, as a bit of curve and wiggle adds interest.

4. Using #8 green pearle cotton, stem stitch down the stem of the flower. Pin the two leaves onto the flower stem, and blanket stitch around the leaves and flower using green and red pearle cotton respectively. Stem stitch the petal on the flower.

5. Sew the three ¼" red buttons at the top of the flower. Secure the buttons with Fray Check.

Construct the bag following the "Bag Construction" instructions on page 65.

Bag Construction

1. Sew the 11½" × 11½" square for the bottom of the bag to the 11½" × 20½" lining rectangle along the 11½" side. Press seam toward the bag lining.

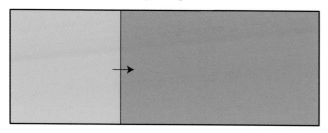

2. Fold the bag right sides together, and sew along the length of the rectangle to create a tube. Be sure to match the seam that joins the bottom of the bag to the lining. Turn right side out, and press the seam to one side.

3. Pull the bottom raw edge of the 11½" square down into the tube so that this raw edge lines up with the raw edge at the opposite end of the tube (lining raw edge). The bag lining is facing outward and the print for the bottom of the bag is now inside the double-sided tube.

Raw edges → 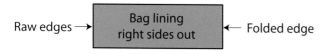 ← Folded edge

Bag lining
right sides out

4. Lay the bag flat with the seam running down the center of the bag. Stitch across the raw edges end of the bag using a ¼" seam.

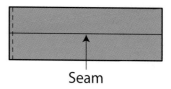

Seam

5. Before turning the bag for the final time, box the bottom corners on both the bag and the lining. Fold the corner so the bottom seam of the bag runs from the point of the corner down the center of the triangle. Using a marking tool of your choice, mark a stitching line 1" from the point of the corner. Stitch across the corner of the bag on the stitching line, backstitching at the beginning and end of the seam line. Trim seam allowance to ¼". Repeat with the second corner.

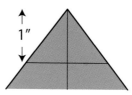
1"

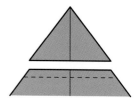

6. Turn right side out.

7. On the bag top, along the seam of the bag, sew the center of a 27" piece of grosgrain ribbon in place using a few small hand stitches. The ribbon should sit ½" above the seam that joins the bottom print to the top print of the bag. Sew a ⅝" decorative button over the ribbon to further secure the ribbon. Add a drop of Fray Check to the thread holding the button in place.

Hopscotch Hint: *If you are using a ribbon that frays badly, cut the ribbon 29" long and tie a small knot at each end of the ribbon.*

Elissa's favorite wine — Barefoot Moscato
Heather's favorite wine — Schmitt Sohne Riesling from Germany

For friends who do not care for wine, don't forget the many wonderful sparkling juices that come in wine bottles!

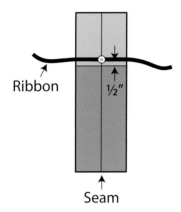

Ribbon   ½"

Seam

8. Cut the ends of the grosgrain ribbon at an angle. Run a line of Fray Check along the cut edge of the ribbon to prevent fraying.

The Stylish Techy – tablet cover

Let your tablet cover make its own fashion statement! Tucked inside this sturdy case, it can be slid into a purse or tote bag for safe travels.

Instructions given are for the leaf tablet cover.

Materials

- One fat quarter of black leaf print for outside of tablet cover
- One fat quarter of cream leaf print for inside of tablet cover
- 6" × 18" of orange for appliquéd band and medallion on flap
- One fat quarter of black for bias binding
- 18" × 20" of black Soft and Stable batting
- 4" × 9" of light weight fusible interfacing for appliquéd band — optional
- 1" × 1½" of black Velcro (use wide, strong Velcro for this project)
- Freezer paper for pattern templates
- Freezer paper or Steam-A-Seam for appliqué

For leaf tablet cover:
- Six 2" × 2" squares of assorted gold and green wool
- #12 black pearle cotton for appliqué
- 10 seed beads for each leaf or tree. (We used rust, gold, silver and cream beads.)

For bird tablet cover:
- 2" × 6" of green, 2" × 2" of blue and 2" × 2" of red tone on tone prints for appliquéd birds
- #12 pearle cotton in green, blue, orange and red for tails, beaks and feet
- Three seed beads for each bird's tail
- Five black seed beads for eyes

Cutting

From rust for appliquéd band and medallion, cut:
1 — 3" × 9" rectangle
1 — 4" square

From black for binding, cut:
2 ¼" wide bias strips — enough for 90" in total when sewn together, end to end, using a 45 degree angle seam.

PROJECT INSPIRATION

Creating the Tablet Cover

Note: *It is important to quilt the fabric before cutting out the front and back of the tablet cover, as the quilting can change the size of the pieces.*

1. Layer the batting between the two leaf prints with the right sides of the leaf prints facing out. Baste and quilt as desired. We quilted a swirl pattern on our leaf cover and a swirl and leaf pattern on our bird cover. Quilt enough of the fat quarter to cut out the rectangles for step 2, OR the whole fat quarter will be quilted.

2. From the quilted fabric created in step 1, cut 1 — 8¾" × 10½" rectangle (front) and 1 — 8¾" × 15" rectangle (back).

3. Trace the curved cutting template found on page 75 onto freezer paper. Cut out the template on the trace lines, and then cut along the curve creating two templates — one with a concave curve (template A) and one with a convex curve (template B).

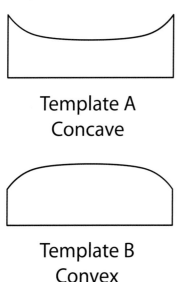

Template A
Concave

Template B
Convex

4. Place the concave template A on the 8¾" edge of the front rectangle, with the outer points of the curve matching up with the corners of the rectangle. Cut along the curved line.

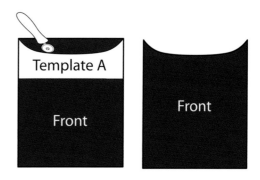

5. Lay the convex template B along the 8¾" side of the back rectangle with the highest part of the curve lined up with the edge of the rectangle. Cut along the curved line.

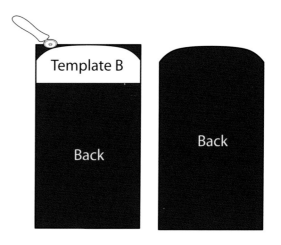

Creating the Appliquéd Band

1. Trace the tree and leaf shapes onto freezer paper, and cut out along the trace line.

2. If desired, iron a 3" × 9" rectangle of lightweight fusible interfacing to the back of the band to add stability.

3. Iron the freezer paper tree and leaf shapes onto the assorted 2" × 2" green and gold wool squares. Cut out the shapes. Pin the leaves and trees in a pleasing arrangement across the 3" × 9" orange rectangle, spacing them evenly across the band. We have given you an extra ⅛" on each end of the band, which you will trim once the band has been sewn in place. Remember there will be a ¼" seam at each end of the band, as well as along the top and bottom of the band.

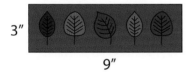

3"

9"

4. Using a blanket stitch, appliqué the 5 leaves and trees in place using #12 black pearle cotton. Using a stem stitch, embroider the stems/trunks and the veins/branches on each motif. Using a coordinating color of thread, sew the seed beads to each motif. Trim the band to 2½" × 8¾".

5. Sew the 2¼" bias binding strips together using a 45 degree angle seam to create one continuous strip. You will need approximately 85" of prepared bias binding for this project. Fold the binding strip in half along the length of the strip, wrong sides together, and press.

6. Cut two 9" lengths of prepared bias binding. On one 9" length of bias binding, open up the binding, and fold the outer edged along the length of the strip into the center of the binding, so that the outer edge meets the fold at the center of the strip. Press in place, and refold the binding along the original fold line.

← Original fold line

7. Sew the double fold bias tape you created in step 6 to the top and bottom of the appliquéd band, tucking the edge of the band into the fold of the bias tape. You will be stitching along the edge of the bias tape that is closest to the center of the appliquéd band.

8. Pin the appliquéd band to the back of the tablet cover positioning it 2½" from the bottom of the rectangle. Stitch in place by topstitching along the outside edge of the bias tape on the band.

2½"

Putting It All Together

1. Sew the remaining prepared bias binding to the concave edge of the tablet cover front. Trim binding even with the sides of the rectangle. Fold over, and slip stitch binding in place.

2. On the front of the tablet cover, position the soft, looped side of the Velcro rectangle ⅛" from the binding. Center the Velcro, and stitch in place. The 1½" side of Velcro should be parallel with the bottom of the front.

⅛"

Outside Front

3. Lay the front of the tablet cover on top of the back with the dark leaf print facing out. Stitch the front to the back, stitching a scant ¼" from the outside edge. Backstitch at the beginning and end of the stitching line.

5. Place the coarse, hooked side of the Velcro on the inside of the tablet flap, ¾" from the binding. Center the Velcro, and stitch in place. The 1½" side of the Velcro should be parallel with the bottom of the tablet front.

4. Bind the outside edge of the tablet cover using the remaining bias binding. Fold over, and slip stitch in place. We chose to sew the binding to the back of the tablet cover and then wrapped it around to the front.

¾"

TRY AN ALTERNATE COLORWAY

6. Appliqué the remaining wool tree in the center of the 4" × 4" orange fabric square using #12 black pearle cotton. Appliqué the trunk and branches on the motif. Using a coordinating color of thread, sew the seed beads to the tree.

7. Trace a circle (found on page 75) onto freezer paper, and cut out on the traced line. Using a light box or a window, center the freezer paper circle on top of the tree appliqué. Press in place. Trim away excess fabric around the circle so that a scant ¼" is showing beyond the freezer paper.

8. Pin the circle to the outside of the flap of the tablet cover, placing it ½" from the flap binding and 3⅝" from each side. It should cover the stitching lines that secure the Velcro to the flap. Appliqué in place.

Hopscotch Hint: *If you do not have time to appliqué and embellish the band on the back of the tablet cover, use a decorative or complimentary print and leave the band plain. You can also use a piece of wide decorative woven ribbon. There are many awesome ribbons on the market.*

Hopscotch Hint: *If you quilted the entire fat quarter for this project, use the left over quilted fabric to create a small change purse or journal cover.*

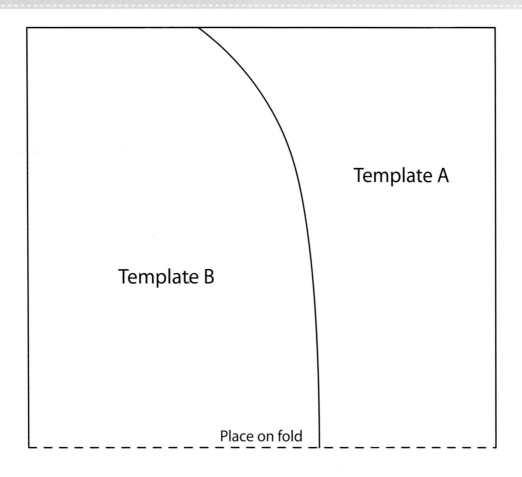

Template A

Template B

Place on fold

That's a Wrap! – cord wrap

Finished Size: Small 4" × 6½" and Large 5" × 8½"

Skill Level:

The idea for our cord wraps came from trying to hide and tidy cords on the coffee counter. Coffee is such an integral part of life at the Willms' household that a whole counter space is devoted to it. The Rancilio (Heather's baby), the Kuerig (Elissa's baby) and the coffee maker all need space along with syrup bottles and espresso cups. Rather than plain utilitarian cord wraps (elastic bands or twist ties), we thought it would be great to spice things up a bit. Laminate cord wraps are great for cords that sit on the floor, like the cord for Heather's Ott light!

PROJECT INSPIRATION

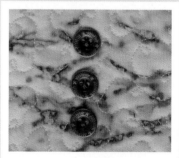

Materials and Cutting

Tan and Red Laminate (small):
- 4" × 6½" cream laminate for front
- 5½" × 8½" red for backing
- 28" of red bias binding or bias tape
- ¾" × 2½" of brown Velcro
- 5½" × 8½" of batting
- One ⅞" brown button
- One ½" red button

Rusted (small):
- 4" × 6½" of rusted fabric for front
- 5½" × 8½" brown print for backing
- 28" of brown bias binding or bias tape
- ¾" × 2½" of brown Velcro
- 5½" × 8½" of batting
- Four ½" metal buttons

Turquoise and Brown (large):
- One 5½" × 5½" orphan block*
- Two 2" × 5½" of brown dot print
- 7" × 10½" of turquoise for backing
- 35" of brown bias binding or bias tape
- ¾" × 3½" of brown Velcro
- 7" × 10½" of batting
- One ¾" turquoise button

Yellow and Gray (large):
- Two 1" × 4½" yellow floral rectangles
- Two 2¾" × 5½" yellow floral rectangles
- Two solid gray 2⅞" × 2⅞" squares
- Two solid yellow 2⅞" squares
- 7" × 10½" yellow floral backing
- 35" of gray bias binding or bias tape
- ¾" × 3½" of white Velcro
- 7" × 10½" of batting

*Hopscotch Hint: *This is a great project to use up orphan blocks. Orphan blocks are left over blocks from previous projects. There is a large bag of them in our studio. The little turquoise and brown block in the large cord wrap was an orphan block. Heather added a 2"-wide rectangle to each end of the block, and the cord wrap was ready for quilting and binding.*

Tan and Red Laminate Wrap

1. Trace the small cord wrap template onto freezer paper. Cut out template on the trace line. Iron the template onto one end of the 4" × 6½" rectangle. Cut out curved corners. Repeat on the other end of the rectangle so that all of the corners are curved.

2. Sandwich the batting between the cream laminate and red prints, right sides facing out.

3. Quilt the cord wrap. We quilted lines of stitching along the length of the wrap. Trim batting and backing even with the cord wrap top.

4. Bind cord wrap with red bias binding. Sew the brown and red buttons to the center of the wrap. Add a dab of Fray Check to the thread used to sew each button in place to further secure the buttons.

5. Using a coordinating color of Velcro, place the soft, loop side of the Velcro rectangle under the right edge of the wrap. Align the long edge of the Velcro with the outside right edge of the wrap, leaving ⅛" between the Velcro and the edge of the wrap. Stitch in place. We stitched around the edge of the Velcro rectangle, backstitching at the beginning and end of our stitching line.

6. Sew the coarse, hook side of the Velcro onto the top left side of the wrap, again aligning the long side of the Velcro rectangle with the outside edge of the wrap, leaving ⅛" between the edge of the Velcro and the edge of the wrap.

Hopscotch Hint: *It is super tricky to get the binding on the small cord wrap, as the longest side isn't really very long. To avoid battling binding in a short space, use a ½" prepared bias tape for the outside. You can make your own using the Clover bias tape makers and have coordinating bias tape while using up left over pieces of fabric.*

Rusted Wrap

1. Cut out curved corners on the rusted fabric following the instructions in step 1 of Tan and Red laminate wrap.

2. Sandwich the batting between the rusted fabric and brown print, right sides facing out.

3. Quilt the cord wrap. We quilted an all-over loop pattern on the wrap. Trim batting and backing even with the cord wrap top.

4. Bind cord wrap with brown bias binding. Sew the three metal buttons to the center of the wrap. Add a dab of Fray Check to the thread used to sew each button in place to further secure the buttons.

5. To sew the Velcro in place, see steps 4 and 5 under Tan and Red laminate wrap.

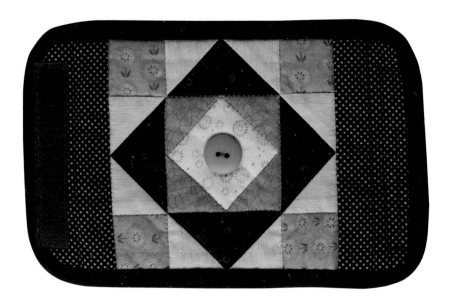

Turquoise and Brown Wrap

1. Sew the 2" × 5½" of brown dot print to the top and bottom of the 5½" × 5½" orphan block. Press seams toward the brown dot print.

2. Cut out curved corners on the pieced top using the large template on page 83 and following the instructions in step 1 of Tan and Red laminate wrap.

3. Sandwich the batting between the pieced top and turquoise print, right sides facing out.

4. Quilt the cord wrap. We stitched in the ditch on the pieced block and quilted parallel lines ½" apart at the top and bottom of the wrap. Trim batting and backing even with the cord wrap top.

5. Bind cord wrap with brown bias binding. Sew the turquoise button to the center of the wrap. Add a dab of Fray Check to the thread used to sew each button in place to further secure the buttons.

6. To sew the Velcro in place, see steps 4 and 5 under Tan and Red laminate wrap.

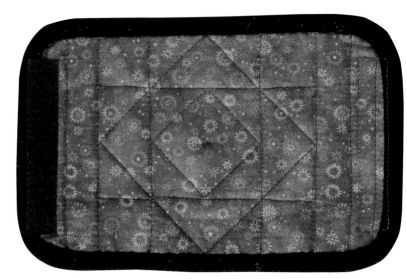

Yellow and Gray Wrap

1. Using a marking tool, draw a diagonal line on the back of both yellow 2⅞" squares.

2. Lay a yellow square on top of a gray square, right sides together. Sew a ¼" seam on both sides of the traced line.

3. Cut along the traced line to create two triangles.

4. Open up the triangles to create two half-square triangle blocks. Press seams toward the gray. Repeat with remaining yellow and gray blocks.

Make 4

5. Sew the four half-square triangle blocks together following the layout diagram below.

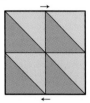

6. Sew a 1" × 4½" yellow floral rectangle to each side of the block. Press seams toward rectangles.

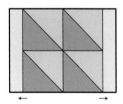

7. Sew a 2¾" × 5½" rectangle on the top and bottom of the pieced unit. Press seams toward 2¾" × 5½" rectangles.

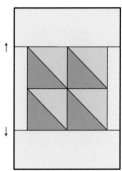

8. Cut out curved corners on the pieced top using the large template on page 83 and following the instructions in step 1 of Tan and Red laminate wrap.

9. Sandwich the batting between the pieced top and yellow floral backing print, right sides facing out.

10. Quilt the cord wrap. We quilted a line of stitching ¼" from the center seam on all of the half-square triangles and parallel lines ½" apart at the top and bottom of the wrap. Trim batting and backing even with the cord wrap top.

11. Bind cord wrap with gray bias binding.

12. To sew the Velcro in place, see steps 4 and 5 under Tan and Red laminate wrap.

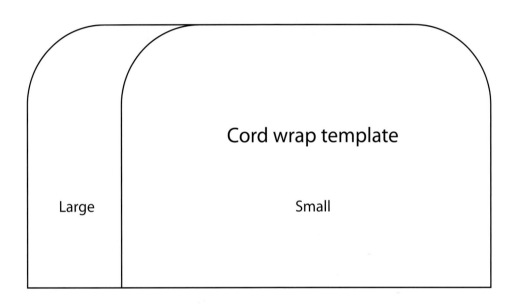

Cord wrap template

Large

Small

Noteworthy —notebook

This versatile little notebook is ideal for sketching, journaling or jotting down random thoughts and lists. Its size makes it perfect for slipping into a purse or backpack pocket. Customize each journal you create by changing the fabrics, paper weights and color combinations.

Materials

- 4 — 8 ½" × 11" text paper*
- 6 ½" × 9 ½" each of two heavy weight prints — the cover can be made from quilting cotton but there are many awesome heavy weight fabrics available and they will create a sturdier cover
- One 6 ½" × 9 ½" lightweight paper for the cover (copy paper would work well here)
- One 1" button
- PVA glue**
- 40 weight thread to contrast or coordinate with the fabric prints (we love King Tut by Superior Threads)
- 13" of heavy cotton thread or twill for book binding
- Fray Check
- Bone folder and awl — optional
- Large-eyed needle

*Text paper is a little heavier than copy paper but not as heavy as card stock
** PVA glue is a strong, white liquid book binder's glue. Other strong liquid glues will work, but this one is ideal because it is archival (it has a neutral or slightly alkaline pH) and strong enough for book binding.

PROJECT INSPIRATION

Creating the Cover

1. Lay one 6½" × 9½" fabric rectangle right side down. Brush a light layer of PVA glue onto one side of the 6½" × 9½" lightweight paper. Place the paper, glue side down, on top of the wrong side of the fabric rectangle. Press in place with your fingers to smooth out any wrinkles or bubbles.

2. Brush a light layer of PVA glue onto the other side of the 6½" × 9½" lightweight paper, which is now facing up. Press the second 6½" × 9½" fabric rectangle wrong side down onto the copy paper. Smooth out any wrinkles or bubbles. You should now have a sandwich of light weight copy paper between two rectangles of fabric, right sides facing out.

3. Set aside to dry (approximately 8 hours).

4. Once dry, using a rotary cutter and ruler, trim to 6" × 9".

5. Stitch the cover using 40 weight thread, following the diagram below. Backstitch at the beginning and end of each stitching line. We stitched ⅛" from the outside all the way around, then we stitched down the center of the journal in both directions. Finally we stitched 2¼" from each 6" outside edge. You may choose to stitch the cover any way you would like. A free motion stitch would be awesome. The stitching is to further secure the layers of the cover together.

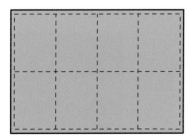

Creating the Signatures

1. Cut the four text papers in half to create eight 5½" × 8½" pieces.

2. Using a bone folder or the edge of the blade of a closed pair of scissors, fold each 5½" × 8½" rectangle in half along the 8½" side. Each rectangle will now measure 5½" × 4¼".

3. Nest the rectangles inside one another to create a signature.

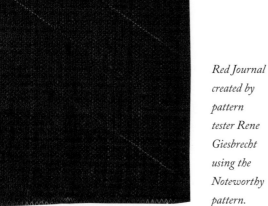

Red Journal created by pattern tester Rene Giesbrecht using the Noteworthy pattern.

Putting It All Together

1. Fold cover in half along the 9" side. The cover now measures 4½" × 6".

2. Open up the cover and lay it flat, with the outside print facing down and the inside print facing up. Lay the signature open on top of the cover, aligning the center of the signature with the center of the journal cover.

3. Use a pencil to mark the hole placement on the top signature paper. To mark the hole placement, make a mark with a pencil ¾" from the top edge of the signature and ¾" from the bottom edge of the signature along the signature fold.

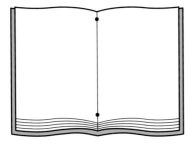

4. Using a large pin or awl, poke a hole through both the signature and the cover at both pencil marks.

5. Using a large-eyed needle and the 13" of binding thread, stitch the signature and journal cover together using the sewing diagram below. Go down at A, leaving a 4" tail. Come up at B, and tie a double knot in the middle of the signature using the 4" tail from where the needle went down at A and the remaining thread on the needle. Place a dab of Fray Check on the knot to secure it further. To avoid getting Fray Check on the paper, slide a small scrap of paper or wax paper under the knot before applying the Fray Check. Let dry.

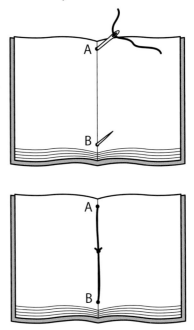

6. Trim excess binding thread to ½", or tie binding thread ends into a bow.

7. Using 40 weight decorative thread, sew the 1" button to the center of the front of the cover. Sew through all layers of the cover. Place a small dab of Fray Check on the thread used to sew the button to the journal cover to further secure the button.

"Either write something worth reading or do something worth writing."
— Benjamin Franklin

Flower Journal created by pattern tester Rene Giesbrecht using the Noteworthy pattern.

Put a Pin in It —pincushion

We like pincushions that are large and heavy enough to stay put, and these ones tick both of those boxes. Filled with crushed granite, they not only keep pins from straying, but they sharpen the pins each time they are placed in the pincushion.

PROJECT INSPIRATION

Materials
- 14" × 16" of felted wool for the body
- 14" × 16" of bi-stretch* interfacing — optional
- 1¾ cups of crushed granite or walnut shells
- Freezer paper

This interfacing is extremely light and maintains some stretch after being adhered to fabric.

Tree:
- 3½" × 3½" cream wool
- #12 cream pearle cotton
- #5 red pearle cotton
- Eight black beads

Bumble Bee:
- 2" × 3" black wool
- 2½" × 3" cream wool
- 3" × 3" yellow wool
- Three black beads for eye and antenna
- #8 black pearle cotton

Cutting

From the felted wool for the body, cut:

2 — 5" × 6" rectangles

1 — 2" × 13¾"

1. Trace the oval shape for the top and bottom of the pincushion onto freezer paper. Transfer all markings to the freezer paper. Cut out oval on the trace line.

2. Iron the freezer paper onto a 5" × 6" rectangle, and cut out the oval. Remove the freezer paper, and repeat for a second oval. Transfer the quarter markings from the freezer paper onto each of the ovals using your favorite marking tool.

Hopscotch Hint: *When pressing the freezer paper onto the wool, be careful to use the tip of the iron, and do not let the iron travel much farther than the freezer paper oval. Ironing may scorch some wool, causing a discoloration where the hot iron has touched the surface of the wool.*

Appliqué Motifs:

Tree

1. Trace the tree shape onto freezer paper, and cut on the traced line.

2. Iron the tree shape onto the 3½" × 3½" cream wool, and cut out. Center and pin the tree onto one black oval.

3. Using #12 cream pearle cotton, blanket stitch the tree to the oval. Draw the branches and trunk onto the tree using a marking tool. Stem stitch the trunk and leaves using #8 red pearle cotton. Sew a bead onto the end of each branch using red thread.

Bumble Bee

1. Trace the bee shapes onto freezer paper, and cut on the traced line.

2. Center and blanket stitch the yellow body to the purple oval using #5 black pearle cotton. Pin and blanket stitch the wings and black stripes to the oval. Using a marking tool, draw the antennas, and embroider using a stem stitch and #5 black pearle cotton. Sew 1 black bead in place for the eye and the remaining 2 beads at the end of each antenna.

Hopscotch Hint: *If you find that your felted wool is not as firm or thick as you would like, at this point iron bi-stretch interfacing onto the back of all three wool pieces. This light weight fusible interfacing will keep the wool soft and pliable but prevent it from stretching with use.*

Creating the Pincushion:

1. Fold the 13 ¾" strip in half creating a loop. Stitch ¼" in from each edge, backstitching for a secure seam. Leave the center of the seam open for turning.

2. Fold the loop in half as pictured above. Place a pin in the fold to mark halfway around the loop. Fold the loop in the opposite direction, lining up the pin and the seam line. Place pins in both of the new folds. You should now have the sides of the pincushion marked in quarters.

3. With right sides together, pin one edge of the loop to the appliquéd oval, matching the markings on the oval with the fold line pins and seam on the loop. Ease into place, and pin around the outside of the oval. Check to be sure the appliquéd surface is facing into the pincushion!

4. Stitch ¼" from the edge, making sure you sew around the entire oval. Do not leave an opening, as you have an opening in the side of the pincushion for turning.

5. Repeat steps 3 and 4, pinning and sewing the second oval to the bottom of the pincushion.

6. Turn the pincushion right side out, gently pulling everything through the opening in the side of the pincushion. It will take a bit of careful tugging, as it is a tight squeeze.

7. Using a funnel, pour the granite through the opening, filling up the pincushion. Make sure that the granite fills the pincushion entirely.

8. Slip stitch the opening closed using coordinating thread!

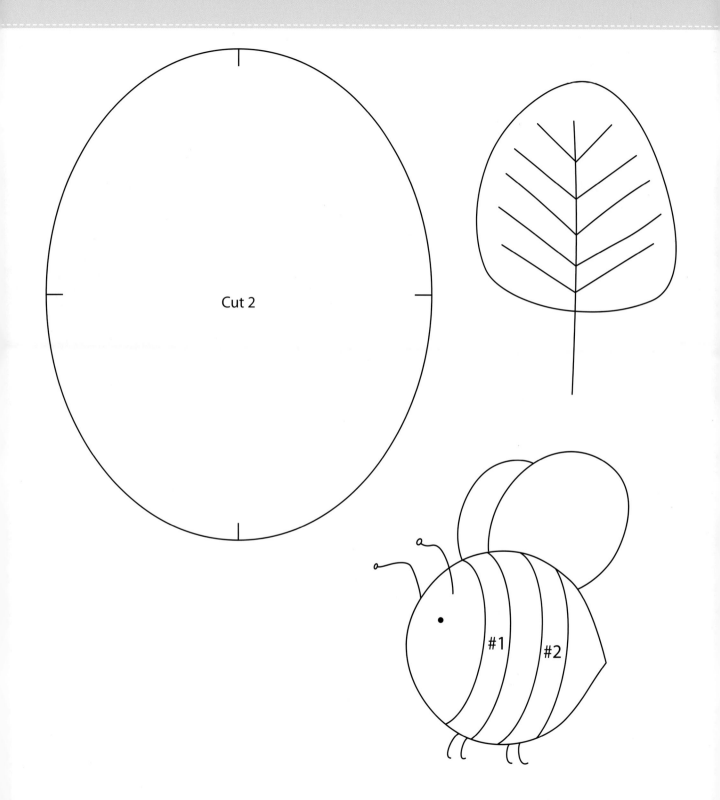

Cut 2

#1 #2

About the Authors

Elissa is a long arm quilter and designer. She enjoys spending her time doing anything artsy, which may include book making, journaling and sketching. Heather is a fifth-grade teacher, and she enjoys engaging her students in the creative process. When not teaching, journaling or reading, she can be found with Elissa in their wonderful studio overlooking Little Ridge "Lake."

Heather and Elissa live in Lethbridge, Alberta. They love traveling, teaching together and meeting other creative souls.

It Takes a Village...

Although it only takes one person to write a book, it takes a village to write a great book. We have an awesome village!

The Kansas City Star:

Thank you for enthusiastically hearing our ideas for this book and including us in every step along the way. We are so glad to be a part of what you do so well.

Kent Richards:

We love that you understood our vision for the book from the very first phone call. Thank you for your many hours of work and your attention to the details that take a book from good to great.

Pattern Testers:

Our pattern testers make our patterns so much better through their valuable input. Thank you Jill Aman, Margo Balzarini, Rene Giesbrecht, Sue Huel, Julianna Huel, Marj Moore and Deb Watson.

Rusted Metal:

Thank you Shawn Gustum and Shirlene Skiba for the unique rusted metal pieces. Such fun to work with!

Heather and Elissa Willms

Materials:

Thank you Jina Barney and Riley Blake for so willingly sharing your amazing fabric with us.

Thank you Bohin for the yummy seam rippers and marking pens for photography.

Thank you Annie Unrein for sharing your Soft and Stable with us. Not only did you send us two packages of Soft and Stable, but this was followed by a whole box! All of which has been put to good use.

Thank you Clover USA for the bias tape makers — tools we now can't imagine living without.